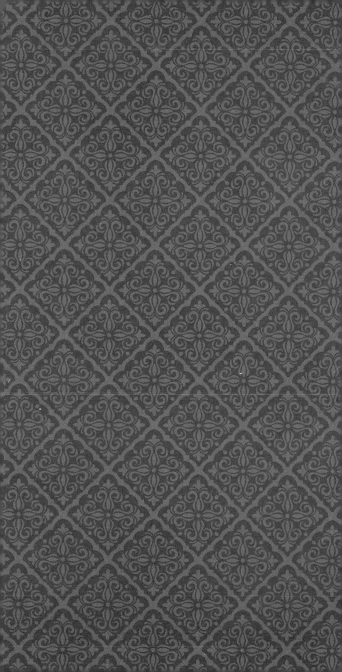

To:

_____

From:

_____

Date:

_____

Published by Christian Art Publishers
PO Box 1599, Vereeniging, 1930, RSA

© 2021
First edition 2021

Designed by Christian Art Publishers

Images used under license from Shutterstock.com

Scripture quotations are taken from the *Holy Bible*,
King James Version, and is in the public domain.

Printed in China

ISBN 978-1-4321-3491-4

21 22 23 24 25 26 27 28 29 30 – 10 9 8 7 6 5 4 3 2 1

Prayers

~ FROM THE ~

·KING JAMES VERSION·

CHRISTIAN ART
PUBLISHERS

Contents

Then shall ye CALL upon me, & YE SHALL GO & pray UNTO ME, & I will HEARKEN UNTO YOU.

JEREMIAH 29:12

What the Bible says about ...

God's Goodness ✦ God's Greatness ✦ Hope
Prayer ✦ Reverence ✦ God's Love
The Will of God ✦ Trusting the Lord
Worship and Praise

God's Goodness

O lord, thou hast searched me, and known me. Thou knowest my downsitting and mine uprising, thou understandest my thought afar off. Thou compassest my path and my lying down, and art acquainted with all my ways.

PSALM 139:1-3

Surely goodness and mercy shall follow me all the days of my life: and I will dwell in the house of the LORD for ever.

PSALM 23:6

I have called upon thee, for thou wilt hear me, O God: incline thine ear unto me, and hear my speech. Shew thy marvellous lovingkindness, O thou that savest by thy right hand them which put their trust in thee from those that rise up against them.

PSALM 17:6-7

God's Greatness

O Lord GOD, thou hast begun to shew thy servant thy greatness, and thy mighty hand: for what God is there in heaven or in earth, that can do according to thy works, and according to thy might?

DEUTERONOMY 3:24

Behold, the LORD our God hath shewed us his glory and his greatness, and we have heard his voice.

DEUTERONOMY 5:24

God thundereth marvellously with his voice; great things doeth he, which we cannot comprehend.

JOB 37:5

GOD'S GREATNESS

For I know that the LORD is great,
and that our Lord is above all gods.

PSALM 135:5

And what is the exceeding greatness of his
power to us-ward who believe, according
to the working of his mighty power, which
he wrought in Christ, when he raised
him from the dead, and set him at his
own right hand in the heavenly places.

EPHESIANS 1:19-20

Now I know that the LORD
is greater than all gods.

EXODUS 18:11

Hope

For thou art my hope, O Lord God:
thou art my trust from my youth.

PSALM 71:5

Let integrity and uprightness
preserve me; for I wait on thee.

PSALM 25:21

For thou wilt light my candle: the LORD
my God will enlighten my darkness.

PSALM 18:28

Heal me, O LORD, and I shall be healed; save
me, and I shall be saved: for thou art my praise.

JEREMIAH 17:14

HOPE

I cried with my whole heart; hear me, O LORD: I will keep thy statutes. I cried unto thee; save me, and I shall keep thy testimonies. I prevented the dawning of the morning, and cried: I hoped in thy word. Mine eyes prevent the night watches, that I might meditate in thy word. Hear my voice according unto thy lovingkindness: O LORD, quicken me according to thy judgment.

PSALM 119:145-149

In the day when I cried thou answeredst me, and strengthenedst me with strength in my soul. All the kings of the earth shall praise thee, O LORD, when they hear the words of thy mouth. Yea, they shall sing in the ways of the LORD: for great is the glory of the LORD. Though the LORD be high, yet hath he respect unto the lowly: but the proud he knoweth afar off. Though I walk in the midst of trouble, thou wilt revive me: thou shalt stretch forth thine hand against the wrath of mine enemies, and thy right hand shall save me.

PSALM 138:3-7

HOPE

*A*nd now, Lord, what wait
I for? my hope is in thee.

PSALM 39:7

*L*et thy mercy, O LORD, be upon
us, according as we hope in thee.

PSALM 33:22

*W*hy art thou cast down, O my soul?
and why art thou disquieted within me? hope
in God: for I shall yet praise him, who is the
health of my countenance, and my God.

PSALM 43:5

*F*or thou art my lamp, O LORD:
and the LORD will lighten my darkness.
For by thee I have run through a troop:
by my God have I leaped over a wall.

2 SAMUEL 22:29-30

Prayer

*A*fter this manner therefore pray ye:
Our Father which art in heaven, hallowed be thy
name. Thy kingdom come, thy will be done in
earth, as it is in heaven. Give us this day our daily
bread. And forgive us our debts, as we forgive
our debtors. And lead us not into temptation,
but deliver us from evil: For thine
is the kingdom, and the power,
and the glory, for ever. Amen.

MATTHEW 6:9-13

*F*or the eyes of the Lord are over the righteous,
and his ears are open unto their prayers.

1 PETER 3:12

*A*nd this is the confidence that we
have in him, that, if we ask any thing
according to his will, he heareth us.

1 JOHN 5:14

PRAYER

The LORD is nigh unto all them that call
upon him, to all that call upon him in truth.
He will fulfil the desire of them that fear him:
he also will hear their cry, and will save them.

PSALM 145:18-19

Ask, and it shall be given you;
seek, and ye shall find; knock, and
it shall be opened unto you.

MATTHEW 7:7

Seek the LORD and his strength,
seek his face continually.

1 CHRONICLES 16:11

The effectual fervent prayer of a
righteous man availeth much.

JAMES 5:16

Rejoice evermore. Pray without ceasing.
In every thing give thanks: for this is the will
of God in Christ Jesus concerning you.

1 THESSALONIANS 5:16-18

PRAYER

Continue in prayer, and watch in the same
with thanksgiving; withal praying also for
us, that God would open unto us a door of
utterance, to speak the mystery of Christ.

COLOSSIANS 4:2-3

Then shall ye call upon me, and ye shall go
and pray unto me, and I will hearken unto
you. And ye shall seek me, and find me, when
ye shall search for me with all your heart.

JEREMIAH 29:12-13

Praying always with all prayer and
supplication in the Spirit, and watching
thereunto with all perseverance
and supplication for all saints.

EPHESIANS 6:18

And all things, whatsoever ye shall ask
in prayer, believing, ye shall receive.

MATTHEW 21:22

PRAYER

And it shall come to pass, that before
they call, I will answer; and while
they are yet speaking, I will hear.

ISAIAH 65:24

If two of you shall agree on earth as touching
any thing that they shall ask, it shall be done
for them of my Father which is in heaven.

MATTHEW 18:19

Whatsoever ye shall ask the Father
in my name, he will give it you.

JOHN 16:23

Therefore I say unto you, what things
soever ye desire, when ye pray, believe that
ye receive them, and ye shall have them.

MARK 11:24

Be careful for nothing; but in every thing
by prayer and supplication with thanksgiving
let your requests be made known unto God.

PHILIPPIANS 4:6

PRAYER

If my people, which are called by my name,
shall humble themselves, and pray, and
seek my face, and turn from their wicked
ways; then will I hear from heaven, and will
forgive their sin, and will heal their land.

2 CHRONICLES 7:14

Whatsoever ye shall ask in my
name, that will I do, that the Father
may be glorified in the Son.

JOHN 14:13

Seek ye the LORD while he may be found,
call ye upon him while he is near. Let the
wicked forsake his way, and the unrighteous
man his thoughts: and let him return unto
the LORD, and he will have mercy upon him;
and to our God, for he will abundantly pardon.

ISAIAH 55:6-7

Reverence

And he said, LORD God of Israel, there is no God like thee, in heaven above, or on earth beneath, who keepest covenant and mercy with thy servants that walk before thee with all their heart: yet have thou respect unto the prayer of thy servant, and to his supplication, O LORD my God, to hearken unto the cry and to the prayer, which thy servant prayeth before thee to day.

1 KINGS 8:23, 28

I will worship toward thy holy temple, and praise thy name for thy lovingkindness and for thy truth: for thou hast magnified thy word above all thy name.

PSALM 138:2

REVERENCE

Now therefore, our God, the great, the mighty, and the terrible God, who keepest covenant and mercy, let not all the trouble seem little before thee, that hath come upon us, on our kings, on our princes, and on our priests, and on our prophets, and on our fathers. Howbeit thou art just in all that is brought upon us; for thou hast done right, but we have done wickedly.

NEHEMIAH 9:32-33

For he that is mighty hath done to me great things; and holy is his name. And his mercy is on them that fear him from generation to generation.

LUKE 1:49-50

Happy is the man that feareth alway: but he that hardeneth his heart shall fall into mischief.

PROVERBS 28:14

God's Love

How precious also are thy thoughts unto me,
O God! how great is the sum of them! if I should
count them, they are more in number than
the sand: when I awake, I am still with thee.

Psalm 139:17-18

Teach me thy way, O Lord; I will walk in
thy truth: unite my heart to fear thy name.
I will praise thee, O Lord my God, with all my
heart: and I will glorify thy name for evermore.
For great is thy mercy toward me: and thou
hast delivered my soul from the lowest hell.

Psalm 86:11-13

I love the Lord, because he hath heard
my voice and my supplications. Because
he hath inclined his ear unto me, therefore
will I call upon him as long as I live.

Psalm 116:1-2

The Will of God

Thou knowest thy servant. O Lord,
for thy servant's sake, and according to thine
own heart, hast thou done all this greatness,
in making known all these great things.
O Lord, there is none like thee, neither
is there any God beside thee, according
to all that we have heard with our ears.

1 CHRONICLES 17:18-20

Therefore now, Lord, let the thing that
thou hast spoken concerning thy servant
and concerning his house be established for
ever, and do as thou hast said. Let it even be
established, that thy name may be magnified
for ever, saying, The Lord of hosts is the God
of Israel, even a God to Israel: and let the house
of David thy servant be established before thee.

1 CHRONICLES 17:23-24

THE WILL OF GOD

Teach me thy way, O Lord; I will walk in thy truth: unite my heart to fear thy name. I will praise thee, O Lord my God, with all my heart: and I will glorify thy name for evermore.

Psalm 86:11-12

Therefore now let it please thee to bless the house of thy servant, that it may continue for ever before thee: for thou, O Lord God, hast spoken it: and with thy blessing let the house of thy servant be blessed for ever.

2 Samuel 7:29

Lord God of Abraham, Isaac, and of Israel, let it be known this day that thou art God in Israel, and that I am thy servant, and that I have done all these things at thy word. Hear me, O Lord, hear me, that this people may know that thou art the Lord God, and that thou hast turned their heart back again.

1 Kings 18:36-37

Trusting the Lord

In thee, O LORD, do I put my trust:
let me never be put to confusion.

PSALM 71:1

And they that know thy name will
put their trust in thee: for thou, LORD,
hast not forsaken them that seek thee.

PSALM 9:10

The LORD is my strength and my shield;
my heart trusted in him, and I am helped:
therefore my heart greatly rejoiceth;
and with my song will I praise him.

PSALM 28:7

What time I am afraid, I will trust in
thee. In God I will praise his word,
in God I have put my trust; I will not
fear what flesh can do unto me.

PSALM 56:3-4

TRUSTING THE LORD

It is better to trust in the Lord than to
put confidence in man. It is better to trust
in the Lord than to put confidence in princes.

PSALM 118:8-9

Unto thee, O Lord, do I lift up
my soul. O my God, I trust in thee:
let me not be ashamed.

PSALM 25:1-2

It is good for me to draw near to God:
I have put my trust in the Lord God,
that I may declare all thy works.

PSALM 73:28

Behold, God is my salvation;
I will trust, and not be afraid: for the
Lord JEHOVAH is my strength and
my song; he also is become my salvation.

ISAIAH 12:2

Worship and Praise

Bless the LORD, O my soul: and all
that is within me, bless his holy name.
Bless the LORD, O my soul, and forget not all
his benefits: who forgiveth all thine iniquities;
who healeth all thy diseases; who redeemeth
thy life from destruction; who crowneth thee
with lovingkindness and tender mercies;
who satisfieth thy mouth with good things;
so that thy youth is renewed like the eagle's.

PSALM 103:1-5

Blessed be the LORD God of Israel from
everlasting to everlasting: and let all the
people say, Amen. Praise ye the LORD.

PSALM 106:48

But I will sacrifice unto thee with the
voice of thanksgiving; I will pay that that
I have vowed. Salvation is of the LORD.

JONAH 2:9

WORSHIP AND PRAISE

I will pray with the spirit, and I will pray with the understanding also: I will sing with the spirit, and I will sing with the understanding also.

1 CORINTHIANS 14:15

Praise ye the LORD. Praise God in his sanctuary: praise him in the firmament of his power. Praise him for his mighty acts: praise him according to his excellent greatness. Praise him with the sound of the trumpet: praise him with the psaltery and harp. Praise him with the timbrel and dance: praise him with stringed instruments and organs. Praise him upon the loud cymbals: praise him upon the high sounding cymbals. Let every thing that hath breath praise the LORD.

PSALM 150

I will sing unto the LORD as long as I live: I will sing praise to my God while I have my being. My meditation of him shall be sweet: I will be glad in the LORD.

PSALM 104:33-34

WORSHIP AND PRAISE

For the LORD is great, and greatly to
be praised: he is to be feared above all
gods. Honour and majesty are before him:
strength and beauty are in his sanctuary.

PSALM 96:4, 6

Blessed be the God and Father of our
Lord Jesus Christ, who hath blessed us with all
spiritual blessings in heavenly places in Christ.

EPHESIANS 1:3

Blessed is the people that know the
joyful sound: they shall walk, O LORD,
in the light of thy countenance. In thy
name shall they rejoice all the day: and in
thy righteousness shall they be exalted.
For thou art the glory of their strength:
and in thy favour our horn shall be exalted.

PSALM 89:15-17

WORSHIP AND PRAISE

Make a joyful noise unto the Lord, all ye lands. Serve the Lord with gladness: come before his presence with singing. Know ye that the Lord he is God: it is he that hath made us, and not we ourselves; we are his people, and the sheep of his pasture.

Psalm 100:1-3

Why art thou cast down, O my soul? and why art thou disquieted within me? hope in God: for I shall yet praise him, who is the health of my countenance, and my God.

Psalm 43:5

Make a joyful noise unto God, all ye lands: sing forth the honour of his name: make his praise glorious. Say unto God, How terrible art thou in thy works! through the greatness of thy power shall thine enemies submit themselves unto thee. All the earth shall worship thee, and shall sing unto thee; they shall sing to thy name.

Psalm 66:1-4

WORSHIP AND PRAISE

O LORD, thou art my God; I will exalt thee, I will praise thy name; for thou hast done wonderful things; thy counsels of old are faithfulness and truth.

ISAIAH 25:1

I will sing of mercy and judgment: unto thee, O LORD, will I sing.

PSALM 101:1

Forasmuch as there is none like unto thee, O LORD; thou art great, and thy name is great in might. Who would not fear thee, O King of nations? for to thee doth it appertain: forasmuch as among all the wise men of the nations, and in all their kingdoms, there is none like unto thee.

JEREMIAH 10:6-7

I will praise the name of God with a song, and will magnify him with thanksgiving.

PSALM 69:30

WORSHIP AND PRAISE

O sing unto the LORD a new song: sing unto the LORD, all the earth. Sing unto the LORD, bless his name; shew forth his salvation from day to day. Declare his glory among the heathen, his wonders among all people.

PSALM 96:1-3

I will praise thee, O LORD my God, with all my heart: and I will glorify thy name for evermore.

PSALM 86:12

I will sing unto the LORD, for he hath triumphed gloriously: the horse and his rider hath he thrown into the sea. The LORD is my strength and song, and he is become my salvation: he is my God, and I will prepare him an habitation; my father's God, and I will exalt him. The LORD is a man of war: the LORD is his name. Who is like unto thee, O LORD, among the gods? who is like thee, glorious in holiness, fearful in praises, doing wonders?

EXODUS 15:1-3, 6, 11

WORSHIP AND PRAISE

O bless our God, ye people, and make the voice of his praise to be heard: which holdeth our soul in life, and suffereth not our feet to be moved. For thou, O God, hast proved us: thou hast tried us, as silver is tried.

PSALM 66:8-10

I will bless the LORD at all times: his praise shall continually be in my mouth. My soul shall make her boast in the LORD: the humble shall hear thereof, and be glad. O magnify the LORD with me, and let us exalt his name together.

PSALM 34:1-3

Bless the LORD, O my soul. O LORD my God, thou art very great; thou art clothed with honour and majesty. Who coverest thyself with light as with a garment: who stretchest out the heavens like a curtain.

PSALM 104:1-2

· BLESS THE LORD, ·

O my soul:

all that is within me,
bless his holy name.
BLESS THE LORD,
O my soul,

&

forget not all his benefits:
who crowneth thee with

· LOVINGKINDNESS ·

AND TENDER MERCIES;
who satisfieth thy mouth
with good things;
so that thy youth
is renewed like the eagle's.

PSALM 103:1-5

When I need ...

A Safe Refuge ✦ Comfort ✦ Forgiveness
Guidance ✦ Help ✦ An Answer to My Prayers
Peace ✦ Protection ✦ Reassurance
Strength ✦ Wisdom

A Safe Refuge

He that dwelleth in the secret place of the most High shall abide under the shadow of the Almighty. I will say of the LORD, he is my refuge and my fortress: my God; in him will I trust. He shall cover thee with his feathers, and under his wings shalt thou trust: his truth shall be thy shield and buckler.

PSALM 91:1-2, 4

Thou art my hiding place; thou shalt preserve me from trouble; thou shalt compass me about with songs of deliverance.

PSALM 32:7

For the LORD is our defence; and the Holy One of Israel is our king.

PSALM 89:18

A SAFE REFUGE

In thee, O LORD, do I put my trust: let me never be put to confusion. Deliver me in thy righteousness, and cause me to escape: incline thine ear unto me, and save me. Be thou my strong habitation, whereunto I may continually resort: thou hast given commandment to save me; for thou art my rock and my fortress. Deliver me, O my God, out of the hand of the wicked, out of the hand of the unrighteous and cruel man. For thou art my hope, O LORD God: thou art my trust from my youth.

PSALM 71:1-5

There is none holy as the LORD: for there is none beside thee: neither is there any rock like our God.

1 SAMUEL 2:2

Unto thee, O my strength, will I sing: for God is my defence, and the God of my mercy.

PSALM 59:17

A SAFE REFUGE

Be thou my strong habitation, whereunto
I may continually resort: thou hast
given commandment to save me; for
thou art my rock and my fortress.

PSALM 71:3

I cried unto thee, O LORD: I said, Thou
art my refuge and my portion in the land
of the living. Attend unto my cry; for I
am brought very low: deliver me from my
persecutors; for they are stronger than I.

PSALM 142:5-6

Thy righteousness is like the great
mountains; thy judgments are a great deep:
O LORD, thou preservest man and beast.
How excellent is thy lovingkindness, O God!
therefore the children of men put their
trust under the shadow of thy wings.

PSALM 36:6-7

Comfort

Blessed be God, even the Father of our Lord Jesus Christ, the Father of mercies, and the God of all comfort; who comforteth us in all our tribulation, that we may be able to comfort them which are in any trouble, by the comfort wherewith we ourselves are comforted of God.

2 CORINTHIANS 1:3-4

The LORD is my shepherd; I shall not want. He maketh me to lie down in green pastures: he leadeth me beside the still waters. He restoreth my soul: he leadeth me in the paths of righteousness for his name's sake.

PSALM 23:1-3

Now our Lord Jesus Christ himself, and God, even our Father, which hath loved us, and hath given us everlasting consolation and good hope through grace, comfort your hearts, and stablish you in every good word and work.

2 THESSALONIANS 2:16-17

COMFORT

Let, I pray thee, thy merciful kindness be for my comfort, according to thy word unto thy servant.

PSALM 119:76

This is my comfort in my affliction:
for thy word hath quickened me.

PSALM 119:50

In thee, O LORD, do I put my trust: let me never be put to confusion. Deliver me in thy righteousness, and cause me to escape: incline thine ear unto me, and save me. Be thou my strong habitation, whereunto I may continually resort: thou hast given commandment to save me; for thou art my rock and my fortress. Deliver me, O my God, out of the hand of the wicked, out of the hand of the unrighteous and cruel man.

PSALM 71:1-4

Sing, O heavens; and be joyful, O earth;
and break forth into singing, O mountains:
for the LORD hath comforted his people,
and will have mercy upon his afflicted.

ISAIAH 49:13

Forgiveness

Who is a God like unto thee, that pardoneth iniquity, and passeth by the transgression of the remnant of his heritage? he retaineth not his anger for ever, because he delighteth in mercy. He will turn again, he will have compassion upon us; he will subdue our iniquities; and thou wilt cast all their sins into the depths of the sea.

MICAH 7:18-19

I acknowledge my sin unto thee, and mine iniquity have I not hid. I said, I will confess my transgressions unto the LORD; and thou forgavest the iniquity of my sin.

PSALM 32:5

See if there be any wicked way in me, and lead me in the way everlasting.

PSALM 139:24

FORGIVENESS

For thou, LORD, art good, and ready
to forgive; and plenteous in mercy
unto all them that call upon thee.

PSALM 86:5

Wash me throughly from mine iniquity, and
cleanse me from my sin. For I acknowledge my
transgressions: and my sin is ever before me.

PSALM 51:2-3

All the paths of the LORD are mercy
and truth unto such as keep his covenant
and his testimonies. For thy name's sake,
O LORD, pardon mine iniquity; for it is
great. What man is he that feareth the
LORD? him shall he teach in the way that
he shall choose. His soul shall dwell at
ease; and his seed shall inherit the earth.

PSALM 25:10-13

FORGIVENESS

And the prayer of faith shall save the sick, and the Lord shall raise him up; and if he have committed sins, they shall be forgiven him.

JAMES 5:15

If we confess our sins, he is faithful and just to forgive us our sins, and to cleanse us from all unrighteousness.

1 JOHN 1:9

But we are all as an unclean thing, and all our righteousnesses are as filthy rags; and we all do fade as a leaf; and our iniquities, like the wind, have taken us away. But now, O LORD, thou art our father; we are the clay, and thou our potter; and we all are the work of thy hand. Be not wroth very sore, O LORD, neither remember iniquity for ever: behold, see, we beseech thee, we are all thy people.

ISAIAH 64:6, 8-9

Guidance

O send out thy light and thy truth:
let them lead me; let them bring me unto
thy holy hill, and to thy tabernacles.

PSALM 43:3

Thy word is a lamp unto my feet,
and a light unto my path.

PSALM 119:105

Cause me to hear thy lovingkindness in
the morning; for in thee do I trust: cause
me to know the way wherein I should
walk; for I lift up my soul unto thee.

PSALM 143:8

Nevertheless I am continually with thee:
thou hast holden me by my right hand.

PSALM 73:23

GUIDANCE

Shew me thy ways, O Lord; teach me thy paths. Lead me in thy truth, and teach me: for thou art the God of my salvation; on thee do I wait all the day. Remember, O Lord, thy tender mercies and thy lovingkindnesses; for they have been ever of old. Remember not the sins of my youth, nor my transgressions: according to thy mercy remember thou me for thy goodness' sake, O Lord.

PSALM 25:4-7

But now, O Lord, thou art our father; we are the clay, and thou our potter; and we all are the work of thy hand.

ISAIAH 64:8

Thou in thy mercy hast led forth the people which thou hast redeemed: thou hast guided them in thy strength unto thy holy habitation.

EXODUS 15:13

For thou art my rock and my fortress; therefore for thy name's sake lead me, and guide me.

PSALM 31:3

GUIDANCE

Lead me, O Lord, in thy righteousness
because of mine enemies; make thy
way straight before my face.

PSALM 5:8

Order my steps in thy word: and let not
any iniquity have dominion over me.

PSALM 119:133

Deliver me, O Lord, from mine enemies:
I flee unto thee to hide me. Teach me to do thy
will; for thou art my God: thy spirit is good;
lead me into the land of uprightness. Quicken
me, O Lord, for thy name's sake: for thy
righteousness' sake bring my soul out of trouble.

PSALM 143:9-11

Hear my cry, O God; attend unto my prayer.
From the end of the earth will I cry unto thee,
when my heart is overwhelmed: lead me to the
rock that is higher than I. For thou hast been a
shelter for me, and a strong tower from the enemy.

PSALM 61:1-3

Help

Bow down thine ear, O Lord, hear me: for I am poor and needy. Preserve my soul; for I am holy: O thou my God, save thy servant that trusteth in thee.

PSALM 86:1-2

But unto thee have I cried, O Lord.

PSALM 88:13

But thou, O Lord, art a shield for me; my glory, and the lifter up of mine head. I cried unto the Lord with my voice, and he heard me out of his holy hill.

PSALM 3:3-4

I will lift up mine eyes unto the hills, from whence cometh my help. My help cometh from the Lord, which made heaven and earth.

PSALM 121:1-2

HELP

I waited patiently for the LORD; and he
inclined unto me, and heard my cry.

For the Lord GOD will help me; therefore
shall I not be confounded: therefore have I
set my face like a flint, and I know that I shall
not be ashamed. He is near that justifieth
me; who will contend with me? let us stand
together: who is mine adversary? let him
come near to me. Behold, the Lord GOD will
help me; who is he that shall condemn me?
who is among you that feareth the Lord, that
obeyeth the voice of his servant, that walketh
in darkness, and hath no light? let him trust in
the name of the LORD, and stay upon his God.

ISAIAH 50: 7-10

The LORD is my strength and my shield;
my heart trusted in him, and I am helped:
therefore my heart greatly rejoiceth;
and with my song will I praise him.

PSALM 28:7

HELP

Make haste, o God, to deliver me; make haste to help me, O LORD. Let them be ashamed and confounded that seek after my soul: let them be turned backward, and put to confusion, that desire my hurt. Let them be turned back for a reward of their shame that say, Aha, aha. Let all those that seek thee rejoice and be glad in thee: and let such as love thy salvation say continually, Let God be magnified. But I am poor and needy: make haste unto me, O God: thou art my help and my deliverer; O LORD, make no tarrying.

PSALM 70:1-5

Hear the right, O LORD, attend unto my cry, give ear unto my prayer, that goeth not out of feigned lips. Thou hast proved mine heart; thou hast visited me in the night; thou hast tried me, and shalt find nothing; I am purposed that my mouth shall not transgress. Hold up my goings in thy paths, that my footsteps slip not.

PSALM 17:1-3, 5

When I Need ...

HELP

I sought the LORD, and he heard me,
and delivered me from all my fears. They
looked unto him, and were lightened:
and their faces were not ashamed. This
poor man cried, and the LORD heard him,
and saved him out of all his troubles.

PSALM 34:4-6

Give ear, O LORD, unto my prayer;
and attend to the voice of my supplications.
In the day of my trouble I will call upon
thee: for thou wilt answer me.

PSALM 86:6-7

LORD, it is nothing with thee to help,
whether with many, or with them that have
no power: help us, O LORD our God; for
we rest on thee, and in thy name we go
against this multitude. O LORD, thou art
our God; let no man prevail against thee.

2 CHRONICLES 14:11

An Answer to My Prayers

Have respect therefore to the prayer of thy servant, and to his supplication, O Lord my God, to hearken unto the cry and the prayer which thy servant prayeth before thee.

2 Chronicles 6:19

But verily God hath heard me; he hath attended to the voice of my prayer.

Psalm 66:19

As for me, I will call upon God; and the Lord shall save me. Evening, and morning, and at noon, will I pray, and cry aloud: and he shall hear my voice.

Psalm 55:16-17

When I Need ...

AN ANSWER TO MY PRAYERS

*A*nd whatsoever we ask, we receive of him, because we keep his commandments, and do those things that are pleasing in his sight.

1 JOHN 3:22

*A*nd let these my words, wherewith I have made supplication before the LORD, be nigh unto the LORD our God day and night, that he maintain the cause of his servant, and the cause of his people Israel at all times, as the matter shall require: that all the people of the earth may know that the LORD is God, and that there is none else.

1 KINGS 8:59-60

*N*ow also when I am old and greyheaded, O God, forsake me not; until I have shewed thy strength unto this generation, and thy power to every one that is to come.

PSALM 71:18

*L*et the words of my mouth, and the meditation of my heart, be acceptable in thy sight, O LORD, my strength, and my redeemer.

PSALM 19:14

AN ANSWER TO MY PRAYERS

My voice shalt thou hear in the morning,
O Lord; in the morning will I direct my
prayer unto thee, and will look up.

PSALM 5:3

One thing have I desired of the Lord, that will
I seek after; that I may dwell in the house of
the Lord all the days of my life, to behold the
beauty of the Lord, and to enquire in his temple.
For in the time of trouble he shall hide me in
his pavilion: in the secret of his tabernacle shall
he hide me; he shall set me up upon a rock.
And now shall mine head be lifted up above
mine enemies round about me: therefore will
I offer in his tabernacle sacrifices of joy; I will
sing, yea, I will sing praises unto the Lord.

PSALM 27:4-6

O Lord, I beseech thee, let now thine ear be
attentive to the prayer of thy servant, and to the
prayer of thy servants, who desire to fear thy name:
and prosper, I pray thee, thy servant this day,
and grant him mercy in the sight of this man.

NEHEMIAH 1:11

Peace

I will both lay me down in peace, and sleep:
for thou, Lord, only makest me dwell in safety.

PSALM 4:8

For God is not the author of confusion,
but of peace, as in all churches of the saints.

1 CORINTHIANS 14:33

Lord, now lettest thou thy servant
depart in peace, according to thy word:
For mine eyes have seen thy salvation,
which thou hast prepared before the face
of all people; a light to lighten the Gentiles,
and the glory of thy people Israel.

LUKE 2:29-32

PEACE

Thou wilt keep him in perfect
peace, whose mind is stayed on thee:
because he trusteth in thee.

ISAIAH 26:3

LORD, thou wilt ordain peace for us: for
thou also hast wrought all our works in us.

ISAIAH 26:12

LORD, lift thou up the light of thy
countenance upon us. Thou hast put gladness
in my heart, more than in the time that their
corn and their wine increased. I will both
lay me down in peace, and sleep: for thou,
LORD, only makest me dwell in safety.

PSALM 4:6-8

And let the peace of God rule in your
hearts, to the which also ye are called
in one body; and be ye thankful.

COLOSSIANS 3:15

Protection

Shew thy marvellous lovingkindness, O thou
that savest by thy right hand them which put
their trust in thee from those that rise up
against them. Keep me as the apple of the eye,
hide me under the shadow of thy wings.

PSALM 17:7-8

Withhold not thou thy tender mercies
from me, O LORD: let thy lovingkindness
and thy truth continually preserve me.

PSALM 40:11

Send thine hand from above; rid me,
and deliver me out of great waters.

PSALM 144:7

When I Need ...

PROTECTION

Though I walk in the midst of trouble,
thou wilt revive me: thou shalt stretch
forth thine hand against the wrath of mine
enemies, and thy right hand shall save me.

PSALM 138:7

Yea, though I walk through the valley of the
shadow of death, I will fear no evil: for thou art
with me; thy rod and thy staff they comfort me.

PSALM 23:4

The LORD is my rock, and my fortress,
and my deliverer; my God, my strength,
in whom I will trust; my buckler, and the
horn of my salvation, and my high tower.

PSALM 18:2

PROTECTION

Thou art my hiding place; thou shalt preserve me from trouble; thou shalt compass me about with songs of deliverance.

PSALM 32:7

I trusted in thee, O LORD: I said, Thou art my God. My times are in thy hand: deliver me from the hand of mine enemies, and from them that persecute me.

PSALM 31:14-15

O LORD my God, in thee do I put my trust: save me from all them that persecute me, and deliver me.

PSALM 7:1

For thou hast been a shelter for me, and a strong tower from the enemy.

PSALM 61:3

PROTECTION

He will keep the feet of his saints, and the wicked shall be silent in darkness; for by strength shall no man prevail. The adversaries of the LORD shall be broken to pieces; out of heaven shall he thunder upon them: the LORD shall judge the ends of the earth; and he shall give strength unto his king, and exalt the horn of his anointed.

1 SAMUEL 2:9-10

The LORD also will be a refuge for the oppressed, a refuge in times of trouble. And they that know thy name will put their trust in thee: for thou, LORD, hast not forsaken them that seek thee.

PSALM 9:9-10

Be merciful unto me, O God, be merciful unto me: for my soul trusteth in thee: yea, in the shadow of thy wings will I make my refuge, until these calamities be overpast.

PSALM 57:1

Reassurance

Blessed be the LORD, that hath given rest unto his people Israel, according to all that he promised. The LORD our God be with us, as he was with our fathers: let him not leave us, nor forsake us. That he may incline our hearts unto him, to walk in all his ways, and to keep his commandments, and his statutes, and his judgments, which he commanded our fathers. And let these my words, wherewith I have made supplication before the LORD, be nigh unto the LORD our God day and night, that he maintain the cause of his servant, and the cause of his people Israel at all times, as the matter shall require.

1 KINGS 8:56-59

REASSURANCE

The LORD is nigh unto all them that call
upon him, to all that call upon him in truth.

PSALM 145:18

Why art thou cast down, O my soul?
and why art thou disquieted in me?
hope thou in God: for I shall yet praise
him for the help of his countenance.

PSALM 42:5

When I cry unto thee, then shall mine enemies
turn back: this I know; for God is for me. For
thou hast delivered my soul from death: wilt
not thou deliver my feet from falling, that I
may walk before God in the light of the living?

PSALM 56:9, 13

He hath remembered his covenant for
ever, the word which he commanded
to a thousand generations.

PSALM 105:8

REASSURANCE

I will praise thee; for I am fearfully and wonderfully made: marvellous are thy works; and that my soul knoweth right well. My substance was not hid from thee, when I was made in secret, and curiously wrought in the lowest parts of the earth.

PSALM 139:14-15

I laid me down and slept; I awaked; for the LORD sustained me. I will not be afraid of ten thousands of people, that have set themselves against me round about.

PSALM 3:5-6

I have declared my ways, and thou heardest me: teach me thy statutes.

PSALM 119:26

Strength

For by thee I have run through a troop:
by my God have I leaped over a wall.

2 SAMUEL 22:30

O LORD God, remember me, I pray
thee, and strengthen me, I pray thee.

JUDGES 16:28

O LORD God, thou hast begun to shew
thy servant thy greatness, and thy mighty
hand: for what God is there in heaven
or in earth, that can do according to thy
works, and according to thy might?

DEUTERONOMY 3:24

STRENGTH

For thou hast girded me with strength
to battle: them that rose up against
me hast thou subdued under me.

2 SAMUEL 22:40

The LORD is my strength and song, and
he is become my salvation: he is my God.

EXODUS 15:2

That he would grant you, according to
the riches of his glory, to be strengthened
with might by his Spirit in the inner man;
that Christ may dwell in your hearts by
faith; that ye, being rooted and grounded
in love, may be able to comprehend with all
saints what is the breadth, and length, and
depth, and height; and to know the love of
Christ, which passeth knowledge, that ye
might be filled with all the fulness of God.

EPHESIANS 3:16-19

Wisdom

My son, if thou wilt receive my words,
and hide my commandments with thee;
so that thou incline thine ear unto wisdom,
and apply thine heart to understanding;
yea, if thou criest after knowledge, and liftest
up thy voice for understanding; if thou seekest
her as silver, and searchest for her as for hid
treasures; then shalt thou understand the fear
of the LORD, and find the knowledge of God.

PROVERBS 2:1-5

O how love I thy law! it is my
meditation all the day. Thou through thy
commandments hast made me wiser than
mine enemies: for they are ever with me.

PSALM 119:97-98

WISDOM

*A*nd now, O LORD my God, thou hast made thy servant king instead of David my father: and I am but a little child: I know not how to go out or come in. And thy servant is in the midst of thy people which thou hast chosen, a great people, that cannot be numbered nor counted for multitude. Give therefore thy servant an understanding heart to judge thy people, that I may discern between good and bad: for who is able to judge this thy so great a people?

1 KINGS 3:7-9

*B*ehold, thou desirest truth in the inward parts: and in the hidden part thou shalt make me to know wisdom.

PSALM 51:6

*S*o teach us to number our days, that we may apply our hearts unto wisdom.

PSALM 90:12

WISDOM

Remove far from me vanity and lies: give me neither poverty nor riches; feed me with food convenient for me.

PROVERBS 30:8

That the God of our Lord Jesus Christ, the Father of glory, may give unto you the spirit of wisdom and revelation in the knowledge of him: the eyes of your understanding being enlightened; that ye may know what is the hope of his calling, and what the riches of the glory of his inheritance in the saints, and what is the exceeding greatness of his power to us-ward who believe, according to the working of his mighty power.

EPHESIANS 1:17-19

Praise the Lord for ...

His Abundant Blessings ◆ His Faithfulness
His Holiness ◆ His Omnipotence
His Salvation ◆ The Work of His Hands

His Abundant Blessings

God be merciful unto us, and bless us; and cause his face to shine upon us. That thy way may be known upon earth, thy saving health among all nations. Let the people praise thee, O God; let all the people praise thee.

PSALM 67:1-3

For thou, LORD, wilt bless the righteous; with favour wilt thou compass him as with a shield.

PSALM 5:12

Ask ye of the LORD rain in the time of the latter rain; so the LORD shall make bright clouds, and give them showers of rain, to every one grass in the field.

ZECHARIAH 10:1

Praise The Lord For ...

HIS ABUNDANT BLESSINGS

Then went king David in, and sat before the
LORD, and he said, Who am I, O LORD God?
and what is my house, that thou hast brought
me hitherto? And this was yet a small thing
in thy sight, O LORD God; but thou hast
spoken also of thy servant's house for a great
while to come. And is this the manner of
man, O LORD God? and what can David
say more unto thee? for thou, LORD God,
knowest thy servant. For thy word's sake,
and according to thine own heart, hast thou
done all these great things, to make thy
servant know them. Wherefore thou art great,
O LORD God: for there is none like thee,
neither is there any God beside thee, according
to all that we have heard with our ears.

2 SAMUEL 7:18-22

Thou crownest the year with thy
goodness; and thy paths drop fatness.

PSALM 65:11

HIS ABUNDANT BLESSINGS

O lord, thou hast searched me, and known me. Thou knowest my downsitting and mine uprising, thou understandest my thought afar off. Thou compassest my path and my lying down, and art acquainted with all my ways. For there is not a word in my tongue, but, lo, O LORD, thou knowest it altogether. Thou hast beset me behind and before, and laid thine hand upon me.

PSALM 139:1-5

Turn again our captivity, O LORD, as the streams in the south. They that sow in tears shall reap in joy. He that goeth forth and weepeth, bearing precious seed, shall doubtless come again with rejoicing, bringing his sheaves with him.

PSALM 126:4-6

HIS ABUNDANT BLESSINGS

The LORD hath done great things
for us; whereof we are glad.

PSALM 126:3

But I will remove far off from you the
northern army, and will drive him into a land
barren and desolate. Fear not, O land; be glad
and rejoice: for the LORD will do great things.
Be glad then, ye children of Zion, and rejoice
in the LORD your God: for he hath given you
the former rain moderately, and he will cause
to come down for you the rain, the former
rain, and the latter rain in the first month.

JOEL 2:20-21, 23

The LORD shall open unto thee his good
treasure, the heaven to give the rain unto
thy land in his season, and to bless all the
work of thine hand: and thou shalt lend unto
many nations, and thou shalt not borrow.

DEUTERONOMY 28:12

HIS ABUNDANT BLESSINGS

Blessed is every one that feareth the LORD; that walketh in his ways. For thou shalt eat the labour of thine hands: happy shalt thou be, and it shall be well with thee. The LORD shall bless thee out of Zion: and thou shalt see the good of Jerusalem all the days of thy life.

PSALM 128:1-2, 5

By thee have I been holden up from the womb: thou art he that took me out of my mother's bowels: my praise shall be continually of thee. I am as a wonder unto many; but thou art my strong refuge. Let my mouth be filled with thy praise and with thy honour all the day.

PSALM 71:6-8

His Faithfulness

Withhold not thou thy tender mercies
from me, O LORD: let thy lovingkindness
and thy truth continually preserve me.

PSALM 40:11

Thy faithfulness is unto all generations: thou
hast established the earth, and it abideth.

PSALM 119:90

I will sing of the mercies of the LORD for
ever: with my mouth will I make known thy
faithfulness to all generations. For I have said,
Mercy shall be built up for ever: thy faithfulness
shalt thou establish in the very heavens.

PSALM 89:1-2

But the LORD is faithful, who shall stablish
you, and keep you from evil. And the LORD
direct your hearts into the love of God,
and into the patient waiting for Christ.

2 THESSALONIANS 3:3, 5

His Holiness

Thou hast a mighty arm: strong is thy hand, and high is thy right hand. Justice and judgment are the habitation of thy throne: mercy and truth shall go before thy face.

PSALM 89:13-14

The LORD reigneth; let the people tremble: he sitteth between the cherubims; let the earth be moved. The LORD is great in Zion; and he is high above all the people. Let them praise thy great and terrible name; for it is holy.

PSALM 99:1-3

Thou answeredst them, O LORD our God: thou wast a God that forgavest them, though thou tookest vengeance of their inventions. Exalt the LORD our God, and worship at his holy hill; for the LORD our God is holy.

PSALM 99:8-9

HIS HOLINESS

Who is like unto thee, O LORD, among the gods? who is like thee, glorious in holiness, fearful in praises, doing wonders?

EXODUS 15:11

There is none holy as the LORD: for there is none beside thee: neither is there any rock like our God.

1 SAMUEL 2:2

And the heavens shall praise thy wonders, O LORD: thy faithfulness also in the congregation of the saints. For who in the heaven can be compared unto the LORD? who among the sons of the mighty can be likened unto the LORD?

PSALM 89:5-6

Give unto the LORD the glory due unto his name: bring an offering, and come into his courts. O worship the LORD in the beauty of holiness: fear before him, all the earth.

PSALM 96:8-9

His Omnipotence

Stand up and bless the LORD your God for ever and ever: and blessed be thy glorious name, which is exalted above all blessing and praise. Thou, even thou, art LORD alone; thou hast made heaven, the heaven of heavens, with all their host, the earth, and all things that are therein, the seas, and all that is therein, and thou preservest them all; and the host of heaven worshippeth thee.

NEHEMIAH 9:5-6

Worthy is the Lamb that was slain to receive power, and riches, and wisdom, and strength, and honour, and glory, and blessing.

REVELATION 5:12

Now unto him that is able to keep you from falling, and to present you faultless before the presence of his glory with exceeding joy, to the only wise God our Saviour, be glory and majesty, dominion and power, both now and ever. Amen.

JUDE 24-25

Praise The Lord For ...

HIS OMNIPOTENCE

Lord, thou art God, which hast made heaven, and earth, and the sea, and all that in them is. And now, Lord, behold their threatenings: and grant unto thy servants, that with all boldness they may speak thy word, by stretching forth thine hand to heal; and that signs and wonders may be done by the name of thy holy child Jesus.

ACTS 4:24, 29-30

Glory ye in his holy name: let the heart of them rejoice that seek the Lord. Seek the LORD and his strength, seek his face continually.

1 CHRONICLES 16:10-11

Now unto him that is able to do exceeding abundantly above all that we ask or think, according to the power that worketh in us, unto him be glory in the church by Christ Jesus throughout all ages, world without end. Amen.

EPHESIANS 3:20-21

HIS OMNIPOTENCE

All nations whom thou hast made shall come and worship before thee, O Lord; and shall glorify thy name. For thou art great, and doest wondrous things: thou art God alone.

PSALM 86:9-10

For I know that the Lord is great, and that our Lord is above all gods.

PSALM 135:5

My substance was not hid from thee, when I was made in secret, and curiously wrought in the lowest parts of the earth. Thine eyes did see my substance, yet being unperfect; and in thy book all my members were written, which in continuance were fashioned, when as yet there was none of them.

PSALM 139:15-16

HIS OMNIPOTENCE

O LORD, our Lord, how excellent is thy name in all the earth! who hast set thy glory above the heavens. Out of the mouth of babes and sucklings hast thou ordained strength because of thine enemies, that thou mightest still the enemy and the avenger. When I consider thy heavens, the work of thy fingers, the moon and the stars, which thou hast ordained; what is man, that thou art mindful of him? and the son of man, that thou visitest him? for thou hast made him a little lower than the angels, and hast crowned him with glory and honour. Thou madest him to have dominion over the works of thy hands; thou hast put all things under his feet: all sheep and oxen, yea, and the beasts of the field; the fowl of the air, and the fish of the sea, and whatsoever passeth through the paths of the seas. O LORD our Lord, how excellent is thy name in all the earth!

PSALM 8

HIS OMNIPOTENCE

O Lord, I have heard thy speech, and was afraid: O Lord, revive thy work in the midst of the years, in the midst of the years make known; in wrath remember mercy. His glory covered the heavens, and the earth was full of his praise. And his brightness was as the light; he had horns coming out of his hand: and there was the hiding of his power.

HABAKKUK 3:2-4

Whither shall I go from thy spirit? or whither shall I flee from thy presence? if I ascend up into heaven, thou art there: if I make my bed in hell, behold, thou art there. If I take the wings of the morning, and dwell in the uttermost parts of the sea; even there shall thy hand lead me, and thy right hand shall hold me.

PSALM 139:7-10

His Salvation

My soul doth magnify the Lord, and my spirit hath rejoiced in God my Saviour.

LUKE 1:46-47

My heart rejoiceth in the LORD, mine horn is exalted in the LORD: my mouth is enlarged over mine enemies; because I rejoice in thy salvation. There is none holy as the LORD: for there is none beside thee: neither is there any rock like our God.

1 SAMUEL 2:1-2

Whosoever shall call on the name of the LORD shall be delivered.

JOEL 2:32

I have trusted in thy mercy; my heart shall rejoice in thy salvation.

PSALM 13:5

The Work of His Hands

O Lord, how manifold are thy works! in wisdom hast thou made them all: the earth is full of thy riches. So is this great and wide sea, wherein are things creeping innumerable, both small and great beasts.

Psalm 104:24-25

Thou art worthy, O Lord, to receive glory and honour and power: for thou hast created all things, and for thy pleasure they are and were created.

Revelation 4:11

But now, O Lord, thou art our father; we are the clay, and thou our potter; and we all are the work of thy hand.

Isaiah 64:8

THE WORK OF HIS HANDS

I know that thou canst do every thing, and that no thought can be withholden from thee. Who is he that hideth counsel without knowledge? therefore have I uttered that I understood not; things too wonderful for me, which I knew not. Hear, I beseech thee, and I will speak: I will demand of thee, and declare thou unto me. I have heard of thee by the hearing of the ear: but now mine eye seeth thee.

JOB 42:2-5

The LORD hath prepared his throne in the heavens; and his kingdom ruleth over all. Bless the LORD, ye his angels, that excel in strength, that do his commandments, hearkening unto the voice of his word. Bless ye the LORD, all ye his hosts; ye ministers of his, that do his pleasure. Bless the LORD, all his works in all places of his dominion: bless the LORD, O my soul.

PSALM 103:19-22

THE WORK OF HIS HANDS

Blessed be thou, LORD God of Israel our father, for ever and ever. Thine, O LORD is the greatness, and the power, and the glory, and the victory, and the majesty: for all that is in the heaven and in the earth is thine; thine is the kingdom, O LORD, and thou art exalted as head above all. Both riches and honour come of thee, and thou reignest over all; and in thine hand is power and might; and in thine hand it is to make great, and to give strength unto all. Now therefore, our God, we thank thee, and praise thy glorious name.

1 CHRONICLES 29:10-13

These wait all upon thee; that thou mayest give them their meat in due season. That thou givest them they gather: thou openest thine hand, they are filled with good. I will sing unto the LORD as long as I live: I will sing praise to my God while I have my being.

PSALM 104:27-28, 33

THE WORK OF HIS HANDS

Thou rulest the raging of the sea: when the waves thereof arise, thou stillest them. Thou hast broken Rahab in pieces, as one that is slain; thou hast scattered thine enemies with thy strong arm. The heavens are thine, the earth also is thine: as for the world and the fulness thereof, thou hast founded them. The north and the south thou hast created them: Tabor and Hermon shall rejoice in thy name.

PSALM 89:9-12

Let the heavens rejoice, and let the earth be glad; let the sea roar, and the fulness thereof. Let the field be joyful, and all that is therein: then shall all the trees of the wood rejoice.

PSALM 96:11-12

Prayers About ...

Compassion • Mercy • Righteousness
Thankfulness • God's Purpose

Compassion

But thou, O Lord, art a God full of compassion, and gracious, long suffering, and plenteous in mercy and truth. O turn unto me, and have mercy upon me; give thy strength unto thy servant, and save the son of thine handmaid. Shew me a token for good; that they which hate me may see it, and be ashamed: because thou, Lord, hast holpen me, and comforted me.

PSALM 86:15-17

It is of the Lord's mercies that we are not consumed, because his compassions fail not. They are new every morning: great is thy faithfulness. The Lord is my portion, saith my soul; therefore will I hope in him.

LAMENTATIONS 3:22-24

Prayers About ...

COMPASSION

O LORD, though our iniquities testify
against us, do thou it for thy name's sake:
for our backslidings are many; we have sinned
against thee. O the hope of Israel, the saviour
thereof in time of trouble, why shouldest
thou be as a stranger in the land, and as a
wayfaring man that turneth aside to tarry
for a night? why shouldest thou be as a man
astonied, as a mighty man that cannot save?
yet thou, O LORD, art in the midst of us, and
we are called by thy name; leave us not.

JEREMIAH 14:7-9

COMPASSION

Seeing then that we have a great high priest, that is passed into the heavens, Jesus the Son of God, let us hold fast our profession. For we have not an high priest which cannot be touched with the feeling of our infirmities; but was in all points tempted like as we are, yet without sin. Let us therefore come boldly unto the throne of grace, that we may obtain mercy, and find grace to help in time of need.

HEBREWS 4:14-17

Hear me when I call, O God of my righteousness: thou hast enlarged me when I was in distress; have mercy upon me, and hear my prayer. O ye sons of men, how long will ye turn my glory into shame? how long will ye love vanity, and seek after leasing? but know that the LORD hath set apart him that is godly for himself: the LORD will hear when I call unto him.

PSALM 4:1-3

COMPASSION

*A*nd now shall mine head be lifted up above mine enemies round about me: therefore will I offer in his tabernacle sacrifices of joy; I will sing, yea, I will sing praises unto the LORD. Hear, O LORD, when I cry with my voice: have mercy also upon me, and answer me. When thou saidst, Seek ye my face; my heart said unto thee, Thy face, LORD, will I seek. Hide not thy face far from me; put not thy servant away in anger: thou hast been my help; leave me not, neither forsake me, O God of my salvation.

PSALM 27:6-9

*L*ORD, thou hast been our dwelling place in all generations. Before the mountains were brought forth, or ever thou hadst formed the earth and the world, even from everlasting to everlasting, thou art God.

PSALM 90:1-2

Mercy

And Jabez called on the God of Israel, saying,
Oh that thou wouldest bless me indeed, and
enlarge my coast, and that thine hand might
be with me, and that thou wouldest keep me
from evil, that it may not grieve me! And God
granted him that which he requested.

1 Chronicles 4:10

Return, O Lord, how long? and let
it repent thee concerning thy servants.
O satisfy us early with thy mercy; that we
may rejoice and be glad all our days.

Psalm 90:13-14

Be merciful unto me, O Lord:
for I cry unto thee daily.

Psalm 86:3

MERCY

I said unto the LORD, Thou art my God:
hear the voice of my supplications, O LORD.

PSALM 140:6

The LORD is good to all: and his
tender mercies are over all his works.

PSALM 145:9

Thou in thy mercy hast led forth the people
which thou hast redeemed: thou hast guided
them in thy strength unto thy holy habitation.

EXODUS 15:13

For we have not an high priest which cannot
be touched with the feeling of our infirmities;
but was in all points tempted like as we are,
yet without sin. Let us therefore come boldly
unto the throne of grace, that we may obtain
mercy, and find grace to help in time of need.

HEBREWS 4:15-16

MERCY

Remember, O LORD, what is come upon us: consider, and behold our reproach. The joy of our heart is ceased; our dance is turned into mourning. The crown is fallen from our head: woe unto us, that we have sinned! For this our heart is faint; for these things our eyes are dim. Thou, O LORD, remainest for ever; thy throne from generation to generation. Turn thou us unto thee, O LORD, and we shall be turned; renew our days as of old.

LAMENTATIONS 5:1, 15-17, 19, 21

Create in me a clean heart, O God; and renew a right spirit within me. Cast me not away from thy presence; and take not thy holy spirit from me. Restore unto me the joy of thy salvation; and uphold me with thy free spirit. Then will I teach transgressors thy ways; and sinners shall be converted unto thee.

PSALM 51:10-13

Prayers About ...

MERCY

Great are thy tender mercies, O LORD:
quicken me according to thy judgments.
Many are my persecutors and mine enemies;
yet do I not decline from thy testimonies.

PSALM 119:156-157

Have mercy upon me, O God, according
to thy lovingkindness: according unto the
multitude of thy tender mercies blot out my
transgressions. Wash me throughly from mine
iniquity, and cleanse me from my sin. Behold,
thou desirest truth in the inward parts: and in
the hidden part thou shalt make me to know
wisdom. Purge me with hyssop, and I shall
be clean: wash me, and I shall be whiter than
snow. Make me to hear joy and gladness; that
the bones which thou hast broken may rejoice.

PSALM 51:1-2, 6-8

MERCY

Now therefore, O our God, hear the prayer of thy servant, and his supplications, and cause thy face to shine upon thy sanctuary that is desolate, for the Lord's sake. O my God, incline thine ear, and hear; open thine eyes, and behold our desolations, and the city which is called by thy name: for we do not present our supplications before thee for our righteousnesses, but for thy great mercies. O Lord, hear; O Lord, forgive; O Lord, hearken and do; defer not, for thine own sake, O my God: for thy city and thy people are called by thy name.

DANIEL 9:17-19

Who is a God like unto thee, that pardoneth iniquity, and passeth by the transgression of the remnant of his heritage? he retaineth not his anger for ever, because he delighteth in mercy. He will turn again, he will have compassion upon us; he will subdue our iniquities; and thou wilt cast all their sins into the depths of the sea.

MICAH 7:18-19

Righteousness

O LORD our God, all this store that we have prepared to build thee an house for thine holy name cometh of thine hand, and is all thine own. I know also, my God, that thou triest the heart, and hast pleasure in uprightness. As for me, in the uprightness of mine heart I have willingly offered all these things: and now have I seen with joy thy people, which are present here, to offer willingly unto thee.

1 CHRONICLES 29:16-17

Create in me a clean heart, O God; and renew a right spirit within me.

PSALM 51:10

Let integrity and uprightness preserve me; for I wait on thee.

PSALM 25:21

RIGHTEOUSNESS

Judge me, O LORD; for I have walked in mine integrity: I have trusted also in the LORD; therefore I shall not slide. Examine me, O LORD, and prove me; try my reins and my heart. For thy lovingkindness is before mine eyes: and I have walked in thy truth.

PSALM 26:1-3

Wherewithal shall a young man cleanse his way? by taking heed thereto according to thy word. With my whole heart have I sought thee: O let me not wander from thy commandments. Thy word have I hid in mine heart, that I might not sin against thee.

PSALM 119:9-11

RIGHTEOUSNESS

*A*nd this I pray, that your love may abound yet more and more in knowledge and in all judgment; that ye may approve things that are excellent; that ye may be sincere and without offence till the day of Christ. Being filled with the fruits of righteousness, which are by Jesus Christ, unto the glory and praise of God.

PHILIPPIANS 1:9-11

*N*either pray I for these alone, but for them also which shall believe on me through their word; that they all may be one; as thou, Father, art in me, and I in thee, that they also may be one in us: that the world may believe that thou hast sent me. And the glory which thou gavest me I have given them; that they may be one, even as we are one: I in them, and thou in me, that they may be made perfect in one; and that the world may know that thou hast sent me, and hast loved them, as thou hast loved me.

JOHN 17:20-23

Prayers About …

RIGHTEOUSNESS

But as for me, I will come into thy house in the multitude of thy mercy: and in thy fear will I worship toward thy holy temple. Lead me, O LORD, in thy righteousness because of mine enemies; make thy way straight before my face.

PSALM 5:7-8

Restore unto me the joy of thy salvation; and uphold me with thy free spirit. Then will I teach transgressors thy ways; and sinners shall be converted unto thee. Deliver me from bloodguiltiness, O God, thou God of my salvation: and my tongue shall sing aloud of thy righteousness. O LORD, open thou my lips; and my mouth shall shew forth thy praise.

PSALM 51:12-15

Thankfulness

Thou sendest forth thy spirit, they are created: and thou renewest the face of the earth. The glory of the LORD shall endure for ever: the LORD shall rejoice in his works.

PSALM 104:30-31

The LORD hath done great things for us; whereof we are glad.

PSALM 126:3

At that time Jesus answered and said, I thank thee, O Father, Lord of heaven and earth, because thou hast hid these things from the wise and prudent, and hast revealed them unto babes. Even so, Father: for so it seemed good in thy sight.

MATTHEW 11:25-26

THANKFULNESS

We give thanks to God and the Father of our Lord Jesus Christ, praying always for you, since we heard of your faith in Christ Jesus, and of the love which ye have to all the saints, for the hope which is laid up for you in heaven, whereof ye heard before in the word of the truth of the gospel; which is come unto you, as it is in all the world; and bringeth forth fruit, as it doth also in you, since the day ye heard of it, and knew the grace of God in truth.

COLOSSIANS 1:3-6

Bless the LORD, O my soul: and all that is within me, bless his holy name. Bless the LORD, O my soul, and forget not all his benefits.

PSALM 103:1-2

Blessed be thy glorious name, which is exalted above all blessing and praise.

NEHEMIAH 9:5

THANKFULNESS

Enter into his gates with thanksgiving, and into his courts with praise: be thankful unto him, and bless his name. For the LORD is good; his mercy is everlasting; and his truth endureth to all generations.

PSALM 100:4-5

Be thou exalted, LORD, in thine own strength: so will we sing and praise thy power.

PSALM 21:13

Praise ye the LORD. I will praise the LORD with my whole heart, in the assembly of the upright, and in the congregation. The works of the LORD are great, sought out of all them that have pleasure therein.

PSALM 111:1-2

THANKFULNESS

I thank my God upon every remembrance of you, always in every prayer of mine for you all making request with joy, for your fellowship in the gospel from the first day until now; being confident of this very thing, that he which hath begun a good work in you will perform it until the day of Jesus Christ.

PHILIPPIANS 1:3-6

I cried by reason of mine affliction unto the Lord, and he heard me; out of the belly of hell cried I, and thou heardest my voice. I went down to the bottoms of the mountains; the earth with her bars was about me for ever: yet hast thou brought up my life from corruption, O LORD my God. When my soul fainted within me I remembered the LORD: and my prayer came in unto thee, into thine holy temple.

JONAH 2:2, 6-7

THANKFULNESS

I will praise thee with my whole heart: before the gods will I sing praise unto thee.

PSALM 138:1

But thanks be to God, which giveth us the victory through our Lord Jesus Christ.

1 CORINTHIANS 15:57

Unto thee, O God, do we give thanks, unto thee do we give thanks: for that thy name is near thy wondrous works declare.

PSALM 75:1

Thou hast caused men to ride over our heads; we went through fire and through water: but thou broughtest us out into a wealthy place. I will go into thy house with burnt offerings: I will pay thee my vows, which my lips have uttered, and my mouth hath spoken, when I was in trouble.

PSALM 66:12-14

God's Purpose

For thou, LORD, hast made me glad through thy work: I will triumph in the works of thy hands. O LORD, how great are thy works! and thy thoughts are very deep.

PSALM 92:4-5

All thy works shall praise thee, O LORD; and thy saints shall bless thee. They shall speak of the glory of thy kingdom, and talk of thy power.

PSALM 145:10-11

The glory of the LORD shall endure for ever: the LORD shall rejoice in his works.

PSALM 104:31

GOD'S PURPOSE

$\mathcal{B}$ecause I will publish the name of the
LORD: ascribe ye greatness unto our God.
He is the Rock, his work is perfect: for all
his ways are judgment: a God of truth and
without iniquity, just and right is he.

DEUTERONOMY 32:3-4

$\mathcal{I}$ will praise thee; for I am fearfully and
wonderfully made: marvellous are thy works;
and that my soul knoweth right well.

PSALM 139:14

$\mathcal{A}$s for God, his way is perfect: the
word of the LORD is tried: he is a buckler
to all those that trust in him.

PSALM 18:30

$\mathcal{T}$he LORD will perfect that which concerneth
me: thy mercy, O LORD, endureth for ever:
forsake not the works of thine own hands.

PSALM 138:8

Prayers About ...

GOD'S PURPOSE

O LORD God of my master Abraham, I pray thee, send me good speed this day, and shew kindness unto my master Abraham. Behold, I stand here by the well of water; and the daughters of the men of the city come out to draw water: and let it come to pass, that the damsel to whom I shall say, Let down thy pitcher, I pray thee, that I may drink; and she shall say, Drink, and I will give thy camels drink also: let the same be she that thou hast appointed for thy servant Isaac; and thereby shall I know that thou hast shewed kindness unto my master.

GENESIS 24:12-14

Ye have not chosen me, but I have chosen you, and ordained you, that ye should go and bring forth fruit, and that your fruit should remain: that whatsoever ye shall ask of the Father in my name, he may give it you. These things I command you, that ye love one another.

JOHN 15:16-17

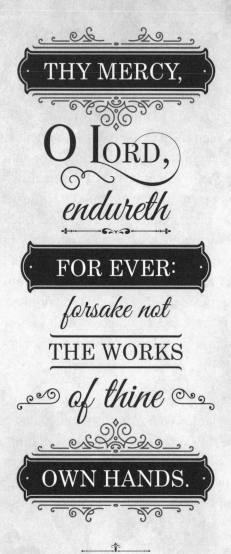

THY MERCY,

O LORD,

endureth

FOR EVER:

forsake not

THE WORKS

of thine

OWN HANDS.

PSALM 138:8

When I Am ...

Afflicted ◆ Ashamed ◆ Blessed by God
Fearful ◆ In Need ◆ Joyful

Afflicted

For thy name's sake, O LORD, pardon mine iniquity; for it is great. Turn thee unto me, and have mercy upon me; for I am desolate and afflicted. The troubles of my heart are enlarged: O bring thou me out of my distresses. Look upon mine affliction and my pain; and forgive all my sins. Consider mine enemies; for they are many; and they hate me with cruel hatred. O keep my soul, and deliver me: let me not be ashamed; for I put my trust in thee.

PSALM 25:11, 16-20

I called upon the LORD in distress: the LORD answered me, and set me in a large place.

PSALM 118:5

AFFLICTED

My God, my God, why hast thou forsaken me? why art thou so far from helping me, and from the words of my roaring? O my God, I cry in the day time, but thou hearest not; and in the night season, and am not silent. But thou art holy, O thou that inhabitest the praises of Israel. Our fathers trusted in thee: they trusted, and thou didst deliver them. They cried unto thee, and were delivered: they trusted in thee, and were not confounded.

PSALM 22:1-5

Give ear to my prayer, O God; and hide not thyself from my supplication. Attend unto me, and hear me: I mourn in my complaint, and make a noise; my heart is sore pained within me: and the terrors of death are fallen upon me. Fearfulness and trembling are come upon me, and horror hath overwhelmed me. And I said, Oh that I had wings like a dove! for then would I fly away, and be at rest. Lo, then would I wander far off, and remain in the wilderness. I would hasten my escape from the windy storm and tempest.

PSALM 55:1-2, 4-8

AFFLICTED

Hear my prayer, O Lord, and let my cry come unto thee. Hide not thy face from me in the day when I am in trouble; incline thine ear unto me: in the day when I call answer me speedily.

PSALM 102:1-2

When I said, My foot slippeth; thy mercy, O Lord, held me up. In the multitude of my thoughts within me thy comforts delight my soul.

PSALM 94:18-19

I will love thee, O Lord, my strength. The Lord is my rock, and my fortress, and my deliverer; my God, my strength, in whom I will trust; my buckler, and the horn of my salvation, and my high tower. I will call upon the Lord, who is worthy to be praised: so shall I be saved from mine enemies.

PSALM 18:1-3, 6

AFFLICTED

In the day when I cried thou
answeredst me, and strengthenedst
me with strength in my soul.

PSALM 138:3

I will extol thee, O LORD; for thou hast
lifted me up, and hast not made my foes
to rejoice over me. O LORD my God,
I cried unto thee, and thou hast healed me.
O LORD, thou hast brought up my soul
from the grave: thou hast kept me alive,
that I should not go down to the pit.

PSALM 30:1-3

And as for me, thou upholdest me in mine
integrity, and settest me before thy face for ever.

PSALM 41:12

Ashamed

O my God, I am ashamed and blush to lift up my face to thee, my God: for our iniquities are increased over our head, and our trespass is grown up unto the heavens. Since the days of our fathers have we been in a great trespass unto this day; and for our iniquities have we, our kings, and our priests, been delivered into the hand of the kings of the lands, to the sword, to captivity, and to a spoil, and to confusion of face, as it is this day. And now for a little space grace hath been shewed from the Lord our God, to leave us a remnant to escape, and to give us a nail in his holy place, that our God may lighten our eyes, and give us a little reviving in our bondage.

Ezra 9:6-8

Blessed by God

The LORD is the portion of mine inheritance and of my cup: thou maintainest my lot. The lines are fallen unto me in pleasant places; yea, I have a goodly heritage.

PSALM 16:5-6

Thou preparest a table before me in the presence of mine enemies: thou anointest my head with oil; my cup runneth over.

PSALM 23:5

Thou openest thine hand, and satisfiest the desire of every living thing.

PSALM 145:16

Both riches and honour come of thee, and thou reignest over all; and in thine hand is power and might; and in thine hand it is to make great, and to give strength unto all.

1 CHRONICLES 29:12

Fearful

Yea, though I walk through the valley of the shadow of death, I will fear no evil: for thou art with me; thy rod and thy staff they comfort me.

PSALM 23:4

Thou drewest near in the day that I called upon thee: thou saidst, Fear not.

LAMENTATIONS 3:57

Be still, and know that I am God: I will be exalted among the heathen, I will be exalted in the earth.

PSALM 46:10

FEARFUL

Then called I upon the name of the LORD; O LORD, I beseech thee, deliver my soul. Gracious is the LORD, and righteous; yea, our God is merciful. The LORD preserveth the simple: I was brought low, and he helped me. Return unto thy rest, O my soul; for the LORD hath dealt bountifully with thee.

PSALM 116:4-7

Then shall thy light break forth as the morning, and thine health shall spring forth speedily: and thy righteousness shall go before thee; the glory of the LORD shall be thy reward. Then shalt thou call, and the LORD shall answer; thou shalt cry, and he shall say, Here I am.

ISAIAH 58:8-9

In Need

How long wilt thou forget me, O LORD? for ever? how long wilt thou hide thy face from me? how long shall I take counsel in my soul, having sorrow in my heart daily? how long shall mine enemy be exalted over me?

PSALM 13:1-2

Then they cry unto the LORD in their trouble, and he bringeth them out of their distresses. Oh that men would praise the LORD for his goodness, and for his wonderful works to the children of men! Let them exalt him also in the congregation of the people, and praise him in the assembly of the elders.

PSALM 107:28, 31-32

IN NEED

Hearken unto the voice of my cry, my King, and my God: for unto thee will I pray.

PSALM 5:2

I will say unto God, Do not condemn me; shew me wherefore thou contendest with me. Is it good unto thee that thou shouldest oppress, that thou shouldest despise the work of thine hands, and shine upon the counsel of the wicked? hast thou eyes of flesh? or seest thou as man seeth? are thy days as the days of man? are thy years as man's days, that thou enquirest after mine iniquity, and searchest after my sin? Thou knowest that I am not wicked; and there is none that can deliver out of thine hand. Thine hands have made me and fashioned me together round about; yet thou dost destroy me.

JOB 10:2-8

When I Am …

IN NEED

Unto thee will I cry, O LORD my rock;
be not silent to me: lest, if thou be silent to
me, I become like them that go down into
the pit. Hear the voice of my supplications,
when I cry unto thee, when I lift up
my hands toward thy holy oracle.

PSALM 28:1-2

My soul thirsteth for God, for the living God:
when shall I come and appear before God?
my tears have been my meat day and night,
while they continually say unto me, Where
is thy God? when I remember these things,
I pour out my soul in me: for I had gone
with the multitude, I went with them to
the house of God, with the voice of joy and
praise, with a multitude that kept holyday.

PSALM 42:2-4

IN NEED

If it had not been the LORD who was on our side, when men rose up against us: then they had swallowed us up quick, when their wrath was kindled against us: then the waters had overwhelmed us, the stream had gone over our soul: then the proud waters had gone over our soul. Blessed be the LORD, who hath not given us as a prey to their teeth. Our soul is escaped as a bird out of the snare of the fowlers: the snare is broken, and we are escaped. Our help is in the name of the LORD, who made heaven and earth.

PSALM 124:2-8

I cried unto God with my voice, even unto God with my voice; and he gave ear unto me. In the day of my trouble I sought the LORD: my sore ran in the night, and ceased not: my soul refused to be comforted. I remembered God, and was troubled: I complained, and my spirit was overwhelmed. Thou holdest mine eyes waking: I am so troubled that I cannot speak.

PSALM 77:1-4

Joyful

Thou wilt shew me the path of life: in thy presence is fulness of joy; at thy right hand there are pleasures for evermore.

PSALM 16:11

For thou, LORD, hast made me glad through thy work: I will triumph in the works of thy hands.

PSALM 92:4

Although the fig tree shall not blossom, neither shall fruit be in the vines; the labour of the olive shall fail, and the fields shall yield no meat; the flock shall be cut off from the fold, and there shall be no herd in the stalls: yet I will rejoice in the LORD, I will joy in the God of my salvation.

HABAKKUK 3:17-18

When I Am ...

JOYFUL

Let all those that put their trust in thee rejoice: let them ever shout for joy, because thou defendest them: let them also that love thy name be joyful in thee.

PSALM 5:11

And the ransomed of the LORD shall return, and come to Zion with songs and everlasting joy upon their heads: they shall obtain joy and gladness, and sorrow and sighing shall flee away.

ISAIAH 35:10

Happy is that people, that is in such a case: yea, happy is that people, whose God is the LORD.

PSALM 144:15

JOYFUL

Verily, verily, I say unto you, that ye shall weep and lament, but the world shall rejoice: and ye shall be sorrowful, but your sorrow shall be turned into joy. And in that day ye shall ask me nothing. Verily, verily, I say unto you, Whatsoever ye shall ask the Father in my name, he will give it you. Hitherto have ye asked nothing in my name: ask, and ye shall receive, that your joy may be full.

JOHN 16:20, 23-24

Rejoice the soul of thy servant: for unto thee, O LORD, do I lift up my soul.

PSALM 86:4

Thy words were found, and I did eat them; and thy word was unto me the joy and rejoicing of mine heart: for I am called by thy name, O LORD God of hosts.

JEREMIAH 15:16

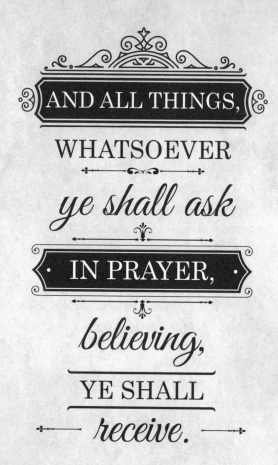

AND ALL THINGS,

WHATSOEVER

ye shall ask

IN PRAYER,

believing,

YE SHALL

receive.

MATTHEW 21:22

Prayers of Faith

David

Who am I, O LORD God? and what is my house, that thou hast brought me hitherto? and this was yet a small thing in thy sight, O LORD God; but thou hast spoken also of thy servant's house for a great while to come. And is this the manner of man, O LORD God? and what can David say more unto thee? for thou, LORD God, knowest thy servant. For thy word's sake, and according to thine own heart, hast thou done all these great things, to make thy servant know them. Wherefore thou art great, O LORD God: for there is none like thee, neither is there any God beside thee, according to all that we have heard with our ears.

2 SAMUEL 7:18-22

Gideon

If now I have found grace in thy sight, then shew me a sign that thou talkest with me. And when Gideon perceived that he was an angel of the Lord, Gideon said, Alas, O Lord God! for because I have seen an angel of the Lord face to face. And Gideon said unto God, If thou wilt save Israel by mine hand, as thou hast said, Behold, I will put a fleece of wool in the floor; and if the dew be on the fleece only, and it be dry upon all the earth beside, then shall I know that thou wilt save Israel by mine hand, as thou hast said. And it was so: for he rose up early on the morrow, and thrust the fleece together, and wringed the dew out of the fleece, a bowl full of water.

JUDGES 6:17, 22, 36-38

Habakkuk

Although the fig tree shall not blossom, neither shall fruit be in the vines; the labour of the olive shall fail, and the fields shall yield no meat; the flock shall be cut off from the fold, and there shall be no herd in the stalls: yet I will rejoice in the LORD, I will joy in the God of my salvation. The LORD God is my strength, and he will make my feet like hinds' feet, and he will make me to walk upon mine high places.

HABAKKUK 3:17-19

Hannah

My heart rejoiceth in the LORD, mine horn is exalted in the LORD: my mouth is enlarged over mine enemies; because I rejoice in thy salvation. There is none holy as the LORD: for there is none beside thee: neither is there any rock like our God. They that were full have hired out themselves for bread; and they that were hungry ceased: so that the barren hath born seven; and she that hath many children is waxed feeble. The LORD killeth, and maketh alive: he bringeth down to the grave, and bringeth up. The LORD maketh poor, and maketh rich: he bringeth low, and lifteth up. He raiseth up the poor out of the dust, and lifteth up the beggar from the dunghill, to set them among princes, and to make them inherit the throne of glory: for the pillars of the earth are the LORD's, and he hath set the world upon them.

1 SAMUEL 2:1-2, 5-8

Jabez

And Jabez called on the God of Israel, saying,
Oh that thou wouldest bless me indeed, and
enlarge my coast, and that thine hand might
be with me, and that thou wouldest keep me
from evil, that it may not grieve me! And
God granted him that which he requested.

1 CHRONICLES 4:10

Jonah

The waters compassed me about, even to the soul: the depth closed me round about, the weeds were wrapped about my head. I went down to the bottoms of the mountains; the earth with her bars was about me for ever: yet hast thou brought up my life from corruption, O Lord my God. When my soul fainted within me I remembered the Lord: and my prayer came in unto thee, into thine holy temple.

Jonah 2:5-7

Jude

Now unto him that is able to keep you from falling, and to present you faultless before the presence of his glory with exceeding joy, to the only wise God our Saviour, be glory and majesty, dominion and power, both now and ever. Amen.

JUDE 1:24-25

Mary

My soul doth magnify the Lord, and my spirit hath rejoiced in God my Saviour. For he hath regarded the low estate of his handmaiden: for, behold, from henceforth all generations shall call me blessed. For he that is mighty hath done to me great things; and holy is his name.

LUKE 1:46-49

Prayers of
Blessing

The LORD make his face shine upon thee, and be gracious unto thee.

NUMBERS 6:25

The LORD God of your fathers make you a thousand times so many more as ye are, and bless you, as he hath promised you!

DEUTERONOMY 1:11

The LORD bless thee, and keep thee.

NUMBERS 6:24

Only the LORD thy God be with thee, as he was with Moses.

JOSHUA 1:17

The LORD lift up his countenance upon thee, and give thee peace.

NUMBERS 6:26

And, behold, as thy life was much set by this day in mine eyes, so let my life be much set by in the eyes of the LORD, and let him deliver me out of all tribulation.

1 SAMUEL 26:24

Blessed of the LORD be his land, for the precious things of heaven, for the dew, and for the deep that coucheth beneath.

DEUTERONOMY 33:13

The LORD deal kindly with you, as ye have dealt with me.

RUTH 1:8

The LORD recompense thy work, and a full reward be given thee of the Lord God of Israel, under whose wings thou art come to trust.

RUTH 2:12

Now the LORD be with thee; and prosper
thou, and build the house of the LORD
thy God, as he hath said of thee.

1 CHRONICLES 22:11

And now the LORD shew kindness and
truth unto you: and I also will requite you this
kindness, because ye have done this thing.

2 SAMUEL 2:6

The LORD shall increase you more
and more, you and your children.

PSALM 115:14

Be of good courage, and let us play the men
for our people, and for the cities of our God: and
the LORD do that which seemeth him good.

2 SAMUEL 10:12

Be of good courage, and let us behave
ourselves valiantly for our people, and for
the cities of our God: and let the LORD
do that which is good in his sight.

1 CHRONICLES 19:13

The LORD hear thee in the day of trouble;
the name of the God of Jacob defend thee.

PSALM 20:1

And the LORD make you to increase and
abound in love one toward another, and
toward all men, even as we do toward you.

1 THESSALONIANS 3:12

Now the Lord of peace himself
give you peace always by all means.
The Lord be with you all.

2 THESSALONIANS 3:16

Traditional
Christian Prayers

Thanks Be to Thee

Thanks be to Thee, my Lord Jesus Christ,
for all the benefits Thou hast won
for me, for all the pains and insults
Thou hast borne for me.
O most merciful Redeemer,
Friend, and Brother,
may I know Thee more clearly,
love Thee more dearly,
and follow Thee more nearly:
for ever and ever.
Amen.

St. Richard of Chichester

Teach Us to Pray

Lord, teach us to pray. Some of us are not skilled in the art of prayer. As we draw near to Thee in thought, our spirits long for Thy Spirit, and reach out for Thee, longing to feel Thee near. We know not how to express the deepest emotions that lie hidden in our hearts. We would not be ignorant in prayer and, like children, only make want lists for Thee. Rather, we pray that Thou will give unto us only what we really need. We would not make our prayers the importuning of Thee, an omnipotent God, to do only what we want Thee to do. Rather, give us the vision, the courage, that shall enlarge our horizons and stretch our faith to the adventure of seeking Thy loving will for our lives. We thank Thee that Thou art hearing us even now. Amen.

PETER MARSHALL

Ordinary Things

I bless Thee, O Father, for all the seemingly
ordinary things – a cup of tea at rising;
a letter through the post;
a bunch of flowers for my vase.
I would not take for granted any gift which
brings me joy – health and strength and good
food; a walk with another in the sunshine;
a favorite book passed on by a friend.
With Paul and people of every generation,
I join in saying that there is nothing
that can separate us – neither height
nor depth; neither life nor death.
Thou are worthy of more love
than I can bring –
accept what I do bring.
Amen.

RITA SNOWDEN

Our Cup of Happiness

Lord God, how full our cup of happiness!
We drink and drink – and yet it grows
not less; but every morn the newly risen sun
finds it replenished, sparkling, overrun.
Hast Thou not given us raiment, warmth and meat,
and in due season, all earth's fruits to eat?
Work for our hands and rainbows for our eyes,
and for our souls the wings of butterflies?
A father's smile, a mother's fond embrace,
the tender light upon a lover's face?
The talk of friends, the twinkling eye of mirth,
the whispering silence of the good green earth?
Hope for our youth and memories for age,
and psalms upon the heaven's moving page?
And dost Thou not of pain a mingling pour,
to make the cup but overflow the more?

Amen.

GILBERT THOMAS

Father, Behold Thy Child

Father, behold Thy child;
Creator, behold Thy creature;
Master, behold Thy disciple;
Savior, behold Thy redeemed one;
Spirit, behold Thy cleansed one;
Comforter, behold one
whom Thou dost uphold;
So I come to Thee, O infinite
and unimaginable,
to worship Thee.
Amen.

MARGARET CROPPER

Desire for God

O Lord our God, grant us grace to desire You
with our whole heart, that so desiring
we may seek and find You,
and so in finding You, may love You,
and loving You, may hate those sins
from which You have redeemed us.
Amen.

Anselm

You Are He

You are the great God – He who is in heaven.
You are the Creator of life,
You make the regions above.
You are the hunter who hunts for souls.
You are the leader who goes before us.
You are He whose hands are with wounds.
You are He whose feet are with wounds.
You are He whose blood is a trickling stream.
You are He whose blood was spilled for us.
Amen.

Give Us, O Lord, a Steadfast Heart

Give us, O Lord, a steadfast heart, which no
unworthy affection may drag downwards;
give us an unconquered heart,
which no tribulation can wear out;
give us an upright heart,
which no unworthy purpose may tempt aside.
Bestow upon us also, O Lord our God,
understanding to know You,
Diligence to seek You, wisdom to find You,
and a faithfulness that may finally embrace You;
through Jesus Christ our Lord.

Amen.

Thomas Aquinas

Lord, Make Me an Instrument

Lord, make me an instrument of Thy peace;
where there is hatred, let me sow love;
where there is injury, pardon;
where there is doubt, faith;
where there is despair, hope;
where there is darkness, light;
and where there is sadness, joy.
O Divine Master, grant that I may not so much
seek to be consoled as to console;
to be understood, as to understand;
to be loved, as to love;
for it is in giving that we receive,
it is in pardoning that we are pardoned,
and it is in dying that we are
born to eternal life.
Amen.

St. Francis of Assisi

Commitment
to Service

Lord Jesus, take me this day and use me.
Take my lips and speak through them.
Take my mind and think through it.
Take my will and act through it,
and fill my heart with love for You.
Amen.

ELIZABETH WALROND

All Creatures Great and Small

Hear our humble prayer, O God,
for our friends the animals,
especially for animals who are
suffering; for all that are overworked
and underfed and cruelly treated;
for all wistful creatures in captivity
that beat against their bars;
for any that are hunted or lost or
deserted or frightened or hungry;
for all that are in pain or dying;
for all that must be put to death:

We entreat for them all Thy mercy and pity,
and for those who deal with them we ask
a heart of compassion
and gentle hands and kindly words.
Make us ourselves to be
true friends to animals and so to
share the blessing of the merciful;
for the sake of Thy Son Jesus Christ our Lord.
*A*MEN.
RUSSIAN PRAYER

Kindness and Mercy

O Merciful Father,
who hath given life to all things
and lovest all that Thou hast made;
pour into the hearts of all men and women
the Spirit of Thine own lovingkindness,
that they may show mercy to all
helpless creatures.
Prosper, we pray Thee,
the efforts of all who are seeking to
prevent unnecessary suffering,
that mankind may glorify Thee by that
gentleness which is according to Thy will;
through Jesus Christ our Lord.
Amen.

ARCHBISHOP CARTER

Bless Our Family

All praise to You, Lord Jesus,
Lover of children:
bless our family,
and help us to lead our children to You.
Give us light and strength,
and courage when our task is difficult.
Let Your Spirit fill us with love and peace,
so that we may help our children to
love You. All glory and praise are Yours,
Lord Jesus, for ever and ever.
Amen.

Lord, Have Mercy

Have mercy, O most
gracious God, upon all men.
Bless especially my father and mother,
my brothers and sisters, my relatives
and friends and all whom I love
or who are kind to me.
Bless also the clergy of this parish,
have pity upon the sick and suffering.
Give us food and clothing, keep us in
good health, comfort us in all our troubles,
make us to please Thee in all we do
and bring us safe at last to our home
in heaven: through Christ Jesus our Lord.
Amen.

CHARLES BOYD

Act of Contrition

O my God,
I am heartily sorry for having
offended Thee, and I detest all my sins,
because I dread the loss of heaven,
and the pains of hell;
but most of all because they offend
thee, my God, who are all good
and deserving of all my love.
I firmly resolve, with the help of Thy grace
to confess my sins, to do penance
and to amend my life.
Amen.

Morning Prayer

Holy, holy, holy, Lord God of Sabaoth;
Heaven and earth are full of
the majesty of Thy glory.
The glorious company of
the apostles praise Thee.
The goodly fellowship
of the prophets praise Thee.
The noble army of martyrs praise Thee.
The holy Church throughout all the
world doth acknowledge Thee,
the Father, of an infinite majesty,
Thine adorable, true, and only Son,
also the Holy Ghost the Comforter.
Amen.

THE BOOK OF COMMON PRAYER

O Merciful God

Be present, O merciful God,
and protect us through the hours of this night,
so that we who are wearied by the
changes and chances of this life
may rest in Your eternal changelessness;
through Jesus Christ our Lord.
Amen.

THE BOOK OF COMMON PRAYER

Prayer for Guidance

Jesus, Savior, pilot me
over life's tempestuous sea;
unknown waves before me roll, hiding rock
and treacherous shoal; chart and compass
come from Thee; Jesus, Savior, pilot me.
Amen.

EDWARD HOPPER

Guide Us

Guide us waking, O Lord,
and guard us sleeping; that awake
we may watch with Christ,
and asleep we may rest in peace.
Amen.

THE BOOK OF COMMON PRAYER

Grant Me, O Lord

Grant me, O Lord my God,
a mind to know You, a heart to seek You,
wisdom to find You, conduct pleasing to You,
faithful perseverance in waiting for You,
and a hope of finally embracing You.
AMEN.

THOMAS AQUINAS

O Merciful God

O merciful God, be Thou unto me a strong
tower of defense I humbly entreat Thee.
Give me grace to await Thy leisure
and patiently to bear what Thou doest unto me;
nothing doubting or mistrusting Thy
goodness towards me: for Thou knowest
what is good for me better than I do.
Therefore do with me in all things what Thou
wilt; only arm me, I beseech Thee with thin
armor that I may stand fast; above all things,
taking to me the shield of faith; praying always
that I may refer myself wholly to Thy will,
abiding Thy pleasure and comforting myself
in those troubles which it shall please Thee to
send to me, seeing such troubles are profitable
for me; and I am assuredly persuaded that
all Thou doest cannot but be well.
And unto Thee be all honor and glory.
Amen.

LADY JANE GREY

The Way, the Truth and the Life

O Lord Jesus,
You have said that You are the Way,
the Truth and the Life.
Suffer us not to stray from You,
who are the way, nor to distrust You
who are the truth, nor to rest
in anything other than You,
who are the life.
Amen.

Desiderius Erasmus

Serenity Prayer

God grant me the serenity
to accept the things I cannot change;
courage to change the things I can;
and wisdom to know the difference.
Living one day at a time;
enjoying one moment at a time;
accepting hardships as the pathway to peace;
taking, as He did, this sinful world
as it is, not as I would have it;
trusting that He will make all things
right if I surrender to His will;
that I may be reasonably happy in this life
and supremely happy with Him
forever in the next.
Amen.

REINHOLD NIEBUHR

Fragrance Prayer

Dear Jesus, help me to spread
Your fragrance everywhere I go.
Flood my soul with Your Spirit and life.
Penetrate and possess my whole being so
utterly, that my life may only be a radiance of
Yours. Shine through me, and be so in me,
that every soul I come into contact with
may feel Your presence in my soul.
Let them look up and see no
longer me, but only Jesus!
Stay with me, and then I shall
begin to shine as You shine;
so to shine as to be a light to others.
Amen.

John Henry Newman

In Christ's Footsteps

The prayers I make will then be sweet
indeed if Thou the spirit give by which I pray.
My unassisted heart is barren clay,
that of its nature self can nothing feed,
of good and pious works Thou art the seed
that quickens only where Thou say'st it may.
Unless Thou show to us Thine own true
way no man can find it: Father!
Thou must lead. Do Thou, then, breathe
those thoughts into my mind by which
such virtue may in me be bred,
that in Thy holy footsteps I may tread;
the fetters of my tongue do Thou unbind
that I may have the power to sing of Thee
and sound Thy praises everlastingly.
Amen.

MICHELANGELO BUONARROTI

Prayer for Integrity

Teach us, good Lord,
to serve You as You deserve:
to give, and not to count the cost,
to fight and not to heed the wounds,
to toil, and not to seek for rest,
to labor, and not to ask for any
reward, except that of knowing
that we do Your will.
Amen.

Ignatius of Loyola

Prayer in Captivity

In me there is darkness, but with You there is
light: I am lonely, but You do not leave me;
I am feeble in heart, but with You there is help;
I am restless, but with You there is peace.
In me there is bitterness, but with You there is
patience; I do not understand Your ways, but
You know the way for me. Lord Jesus Christ,
You were poor and in distress, a captive and
forsaken as I am. You know all man's troubles;
You abide with me when all men fail me;
You remember and seek me; it is Your will
that I should know You and turn to You.
Lord, I hear Your call and follow; help me.

Amen.

DIETRICH BONHOEFFER

Prayer for Consecration

$\sim\!\!\!\text{\textcircled{$\circ$}}\!\!\!\sim$

Use me, my Savior, for whatever
purpose and in whatever way You may
require. Here is my poor heart,
an empty vessel: fill it with Your grace.
Here is my sinful and troubled soul; quicken
it and freshen it with Your love. Take my heart
for Your abode; my mouth to spread abroad
the glory of Your name; my love and all my
powers for the advancement of Your believing
people, and never allow the steadfastness
and confidence of my faith to abate.

Amen.

Dwight L. Moody

Give Us Grace

Give us grace, Almighty Father, to address
You with all our hearts as well as with our lips.
You are present everywhere:
from You no secrets can be hidden.
Teach us to fix our thoughts on You,
reverently and with love,
so that our prayers are not in vain,
but are acceptable to You, now and
always, through Jesus Christ our Lord.
Amen.

JANE AUSTIN

Prayer for Patience

Dear Father,
Give me the patience I need
to wait for Your promises
and the spiritual maturity
to know unequivocally
that You know best.
Amen.

EVELYN CHRISTENSON

Lord, Show Me How

If I can do some good today,
if I can serve along life's way,
if I can something helpful say,
Lord, show me how.

If I can right a human wrong,
if I can help to make one strong,
if I can cheer with smile or song,
Lord, show me how.

If I can aid one in distress,
if I can make a burden less,
if I can spread more happiness,
Lord, show me how.
Amen.

GRENVILLE KLEISER

This New Day

My God, I give You this day.
I offer You, now, all of the good that
I shall do and I promise to accept,
for the love of You, all the
difficulty that I shall meet.
Help me to conduct myself
during this day in a manner
pleasing to You.
Amen.

St. Francis de Sales

Family Prayer

God, give our household the same sweet
harmony I hear in the birds' songs.
Stabilize and strengthen our families.
Restore the sanctity of marriage.
Let parents demonstrate a respect and love
for each other that children may imitate.
Keep us from indulging our children,
confusing material excess
with spiritual necessity.
Soothe the occasional ruffled feathers,
and teach us to live in blessed concert.
Amen.

MARSHA MAURER

Through the Storm

Take my hand, precious Lord
lead me on, let me stand.
I am tired, I am weak, I am worn.
Through the storm, through the
night, lead me on to the light.
Take my hand, precious Lord,
lead me home.
Amen.

THOMAS DORSEY

A Pure Heart

Father, listen to my prayer.
Turn my ways to Your ways; make me holy,
set my thinking right; straighten out my
desires; create a pure heart within me;
give me a new and steadfast spirit.

Amen.

LAUNCELOT ANDREWES

Living Water

Lord, You know the longings of my heart.
When I seek thrills and quick fixes to satisfy
these needs I am eventually disappointed.
Your supply of Living Water never runs dry
and satisfies the inner desires of my heart
because You are the only One who
can meet my spiritual needs.
Lord, as I come today dry and thirsty
I look to You, for You satisfy the thirsty
and fill the hungry with good things.
Amen.

Time

Lord, I have time,
I have plenty of time,
all the time that You give me,
the years of my life,
the days of my years, the hours
of my days, they are all mine.
Mine to fill, quietly, calmly,
but to fill up completely to the
brim, to offer them to You,
that out of their insipid water
You may make a rich wine
as You once made in Cana of Galilee.
I am not asking You tonight, Lord,
for time to do this and then that,
but Your grace to do conscientiously,
in the time that You give me,
what You want me to do.
Amen.

MICHEL QUOIST

At Close of Day

Now the day is over night is drawing nigh,
shadows of the evening steal across the sky.
Jesus, give the weary calm and sweet repose;
With Thy tend'rest blessing
may our eyelids close.
When the morning wakens then may I arrive
pure and fresh and sinless in Thy holy eyes.
Amen.

Sabine Baring-Gould

Wise Words
About Prayer

What can be more excellent than prayer;
what is more profitable to our life;
what sweeter to our souls; what more sublime,
in the course of our whole life,
than the practice of prayer!

St. Augustine

Prayer opens the heart to God,
and it is the means by which the soul,
though empty, is filled by God.

John Bunyan

Keep praying to get a perfect
understanding of God Himself.

Oswald Chambers

I have so much to do that I spend several hours in prayer before I am able to do it.
MARTIN LUTHER

Prayer is not monologue, but dialogue. God's voice in response to mine is its most essential part.
ANDREW MURRAY

Prayer is that act in Christianity in which there is the greatest encouragement.
J. C. RYLE

To pray is to mount on eagle's wings above the clouds and get into the clear heaven where God dwells.
CHARLES H. SPURGEON

Is prayer your steering wheel
or your spare tire?
CORRIE TEN BOOM

The more you pray, the easier it becomes.
The easier it becomes, the more you will pray.
MOTHER TERESA

God does nothing but by prayer,
and everything with it.
JOHN WESLEY

Let
my prayer

· BE SET FORTH ·

before thee

as incense;

&

· THE LIFTING UP ·

of my hands
as the

EVENING

sacrifice.

PSALM 141:2